Taro Gomi's
PLAYFUL PUZZLES for LITTLE HANDS

Taro Gomi's
PLAYFUL PUZZLES for LITTLE HANDS

More than 60 guessing games, twisty mazes,
logic puzzles, and more!

chronicle books·san francisco

Let's play hide-and-seek!

Can you find everyone?

My cat is brown, black, and gray. It has short whiskers and a black tip on its tail. Can you see it?

Which snake is longest? Which is shortest?
Count their sections to find out.

This is what my toy alligator should look like—but there's a piece missing! Can you tell which one?

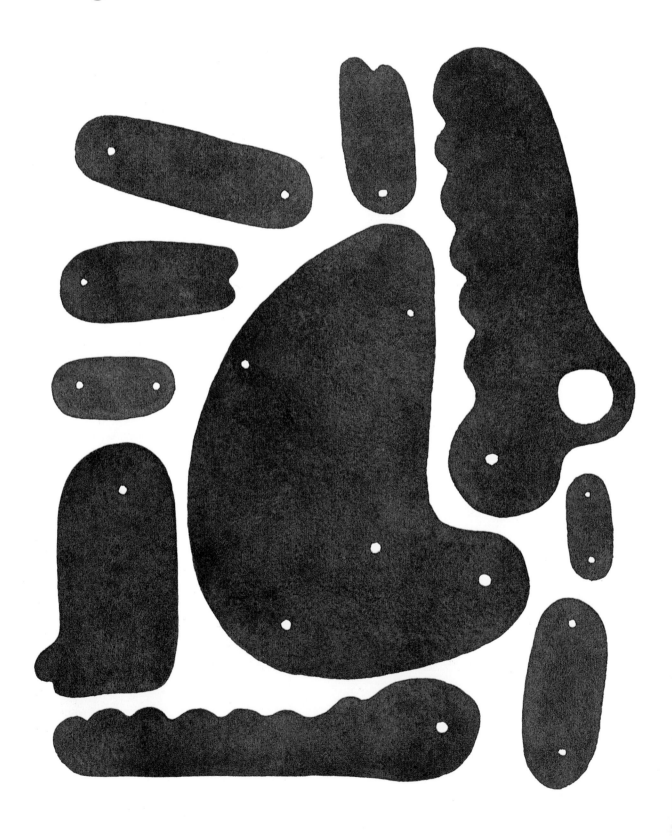

Can you find all of these parts on the alligator?

Yuck! What terrible monsters.
Quick! Cover each of them with one of your hands.

You'll need both hands for this one.

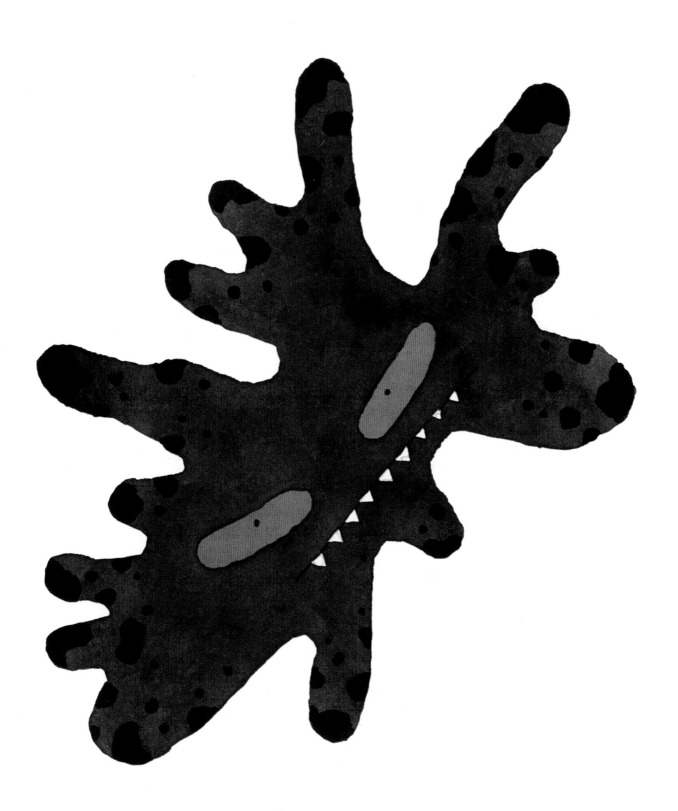

Find the two children who have blue hats with green pom-poms.

Who is playing with the girl wearing a pink and a purple hat?

How many children have a flag?

These are the children
in my school.

**My best friend is second from the
bottom and third from the left.**

Which piece isn't a part of the picture?

Many people live in this apartment building.
My friend Jake's window is on the fifth floor,
fifth room from the right.

Olivia's window is on
the third floor, seventh
from the left.

Noah's window is in
the exact middle of
the seventh floor.

Can you find them all?

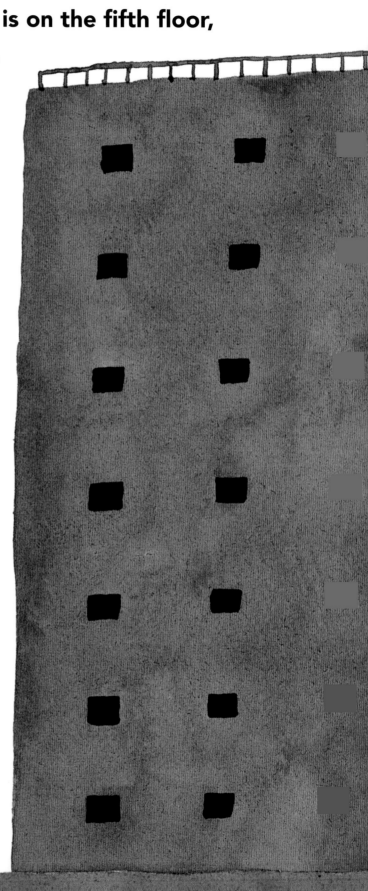

I took a picture of part of the town!

Can you see which part?

How many flowers are pink?
How many are yellow?

Are there more of one color?

Each child had

How many doughnuts did each child eat?

Yum! Strawberries!
How many berries can each child have?

Who has the most?

The child in blue has the most apples.
But what if the apples were worth different points?

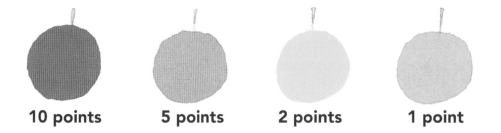

10 points   5 points   2 points   1 point

Who has the most points?

You need ten pieces of bread.

Which pans will you take if you
can take only two pans?

Which pans will you take if you
can take only three pans?

Which pans will you take if you
can take only four pans?

What's wrong with this **shadow?**
How many differences can you find?

Can you find the **differences?**

I cut a flower out for you!

But wait . . . can you spot the differences?

Which one is my toy?

Which clown has more juggling balls?

I made a robot out of blocks!
Which 3 blocks did I not use?

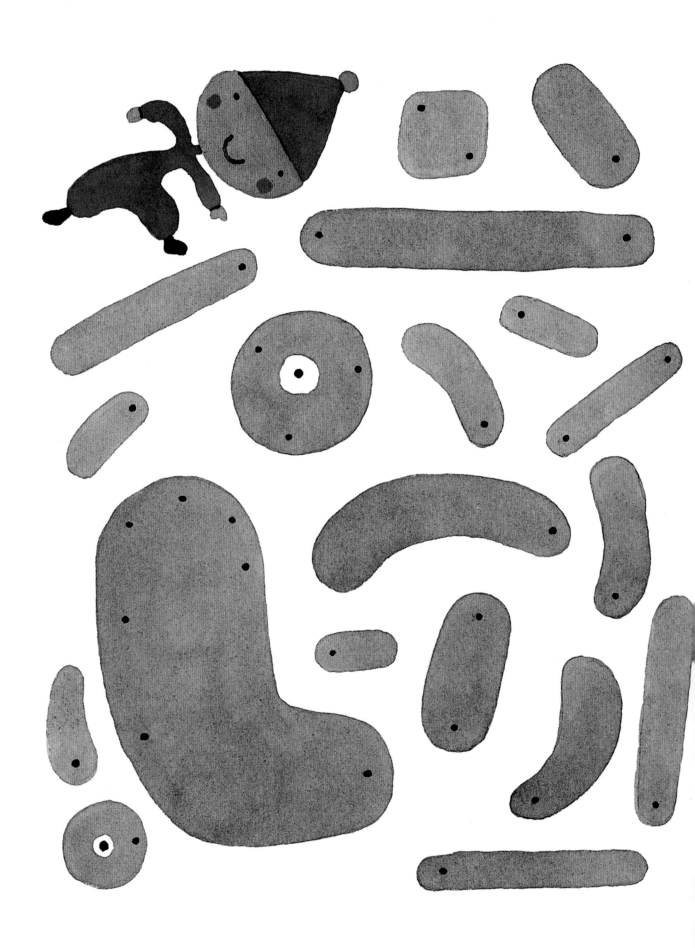

You can make this bird from these pieces!

But there will be some pieces left over—which ones?

How many balls are
the same as mine?

**We can make this rocket
out of these pieces!**

But which two pieces
won't we use?

Which house did I paint a picture of?

Can you find my twin in this crowd?

Whose outline is this?

Which car is the same as mine?

Which one is just like my rocket?
Look carefully!

Two of these have the same pattern.
Which ones?

Ooooo!
Which white ghost shape is the same as the black one?

Which of these children is the one wearing the **mask?**

I cut away part of this square.
Can you find the other part?

Find the two balloons that are the same.

Put one finger on one starting point and another finger on the other starting point.

Can you move them both along their paths at the same time, so they meet in the middle?

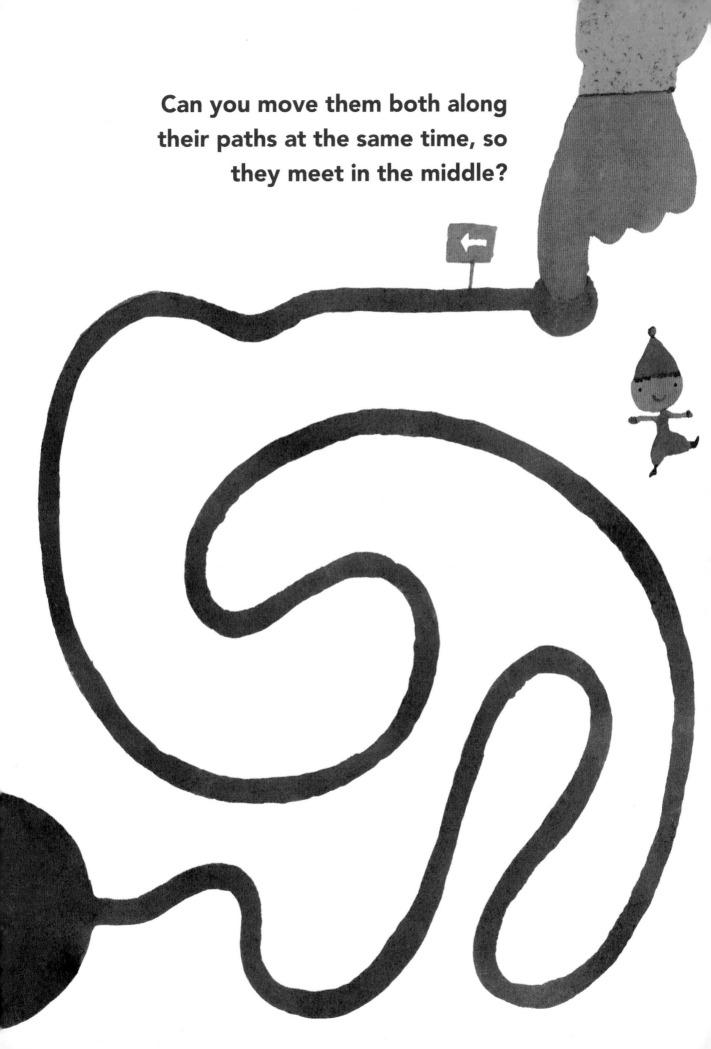

You can step only on the
red and **green** squares.

You cannot move diagonally.
Can you get all the way across?

Let's go for a walk with our fingers.

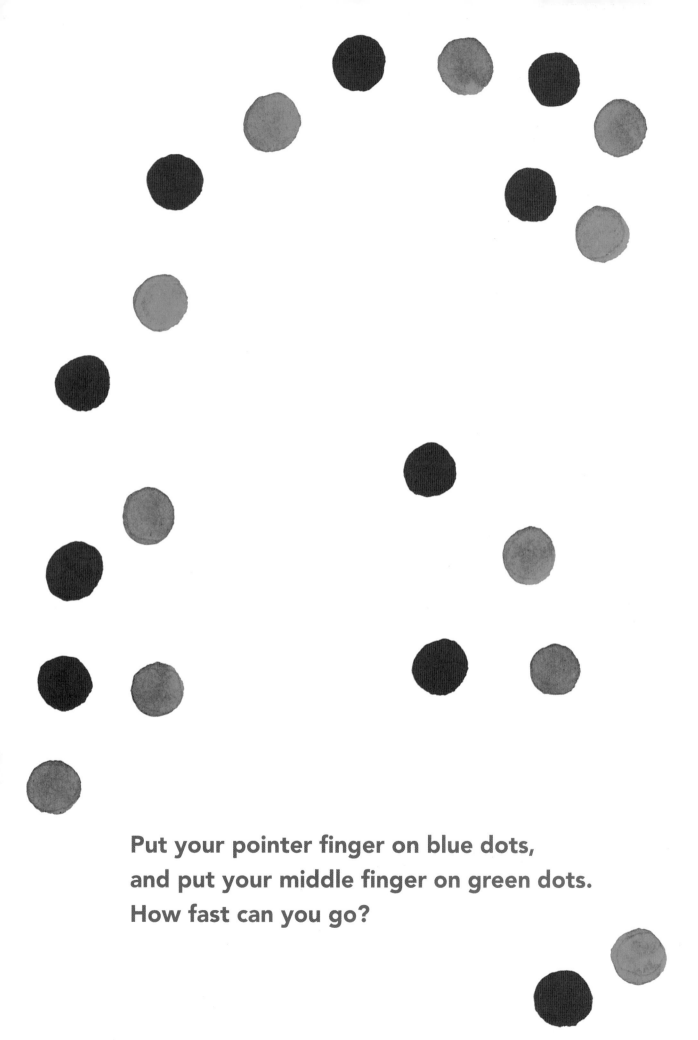

**Put your pointer finger on blue dots,
and put your middle finger on green dots.
How fast can you go?**

What's the shortest path between them?

One starts from the left and one starts from the right. **WHERE WILL THEY MEET?**

What's the shortest way to the top?
What's the longest?

Let's go for a walk with our finger.

Start here.

Go around three times.

Hop back to the start.

STOP!

Can you show him
the way home?

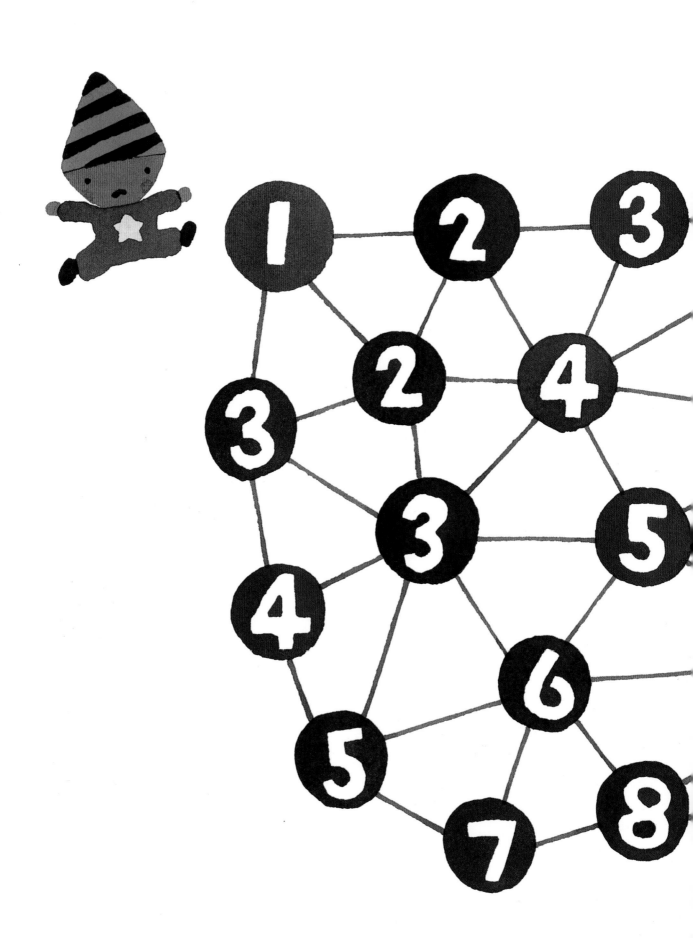

Count from one to ten to find your way through the maze!

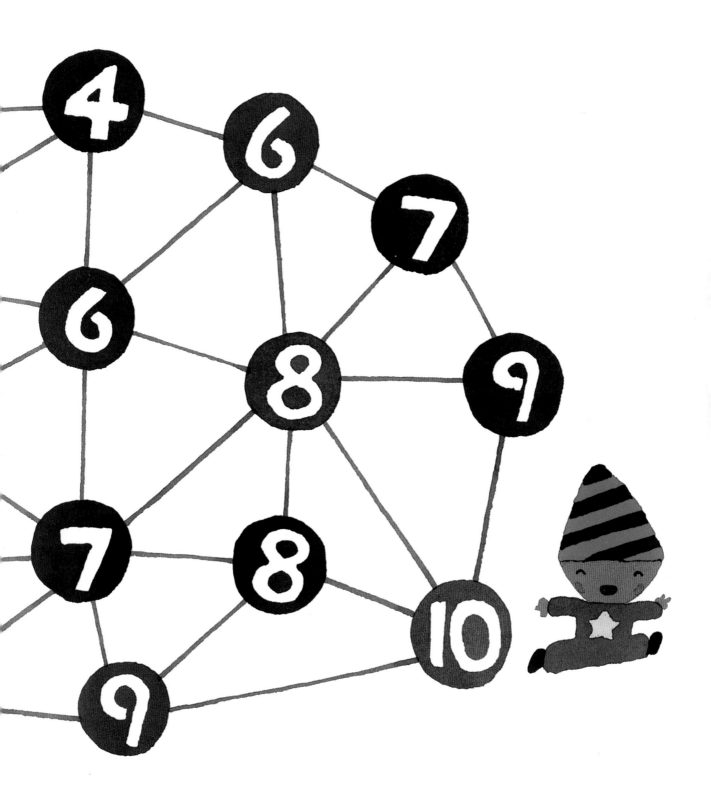

Bring the lost puppy home!

Can you find your way through without passing a house with a blue roof?

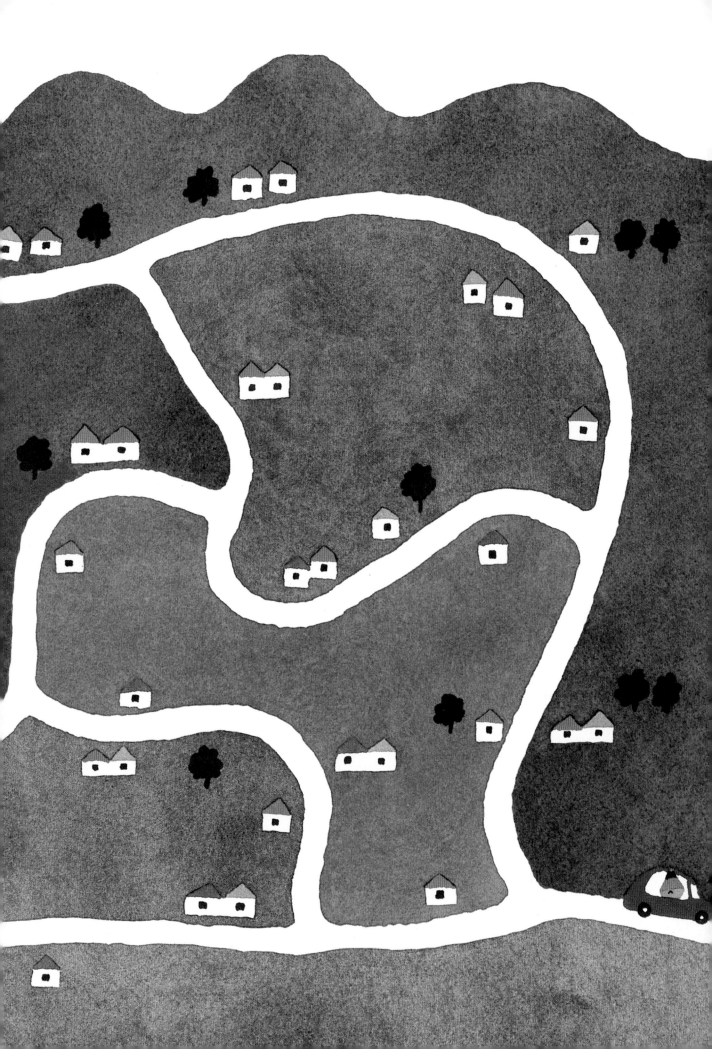

GOAL

Where will the water come out?

What number should be on the cube?
What number should be on the cylinder?

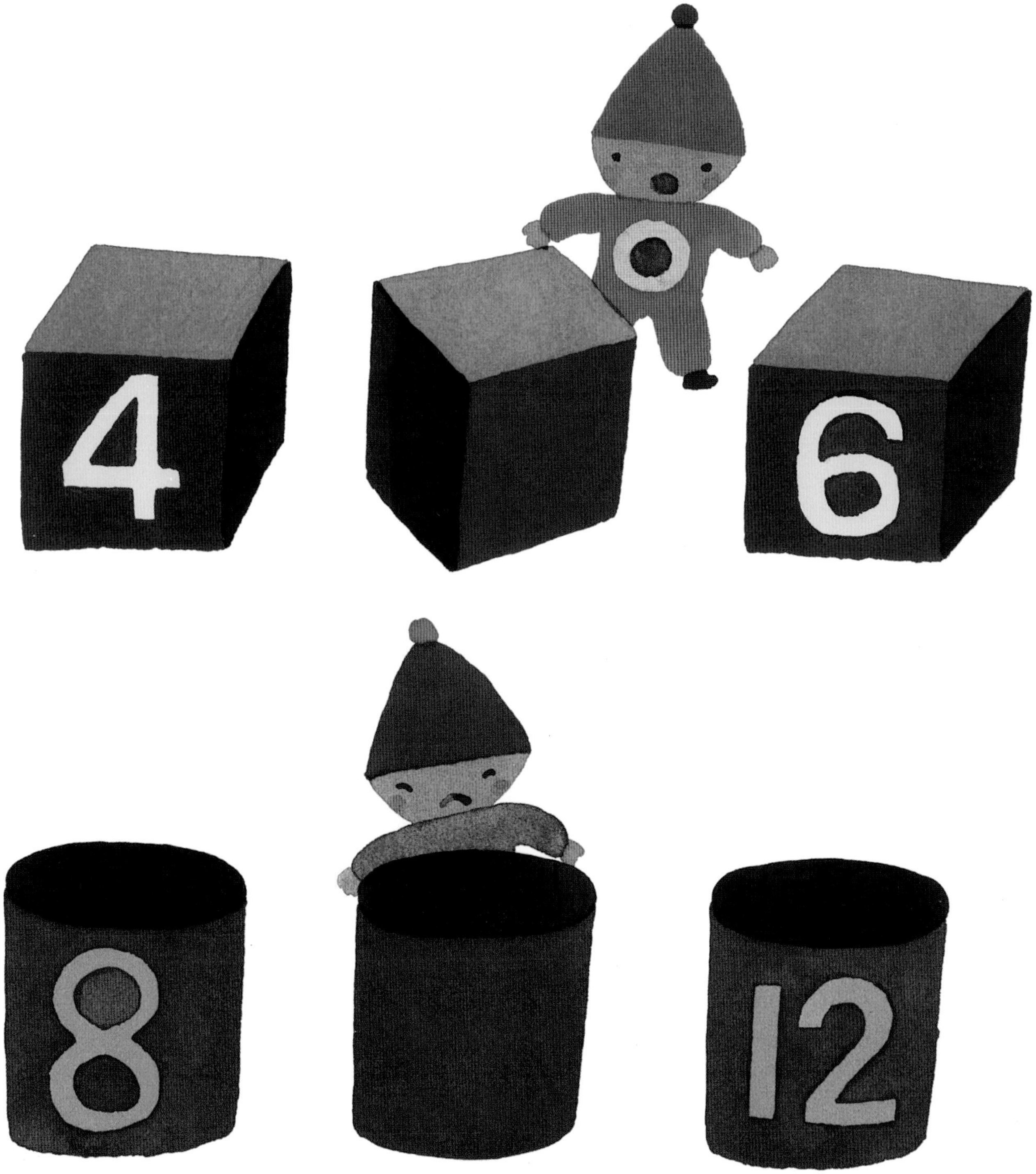
4
6
8
12

Add up the numbers you pass.

Which path will add up to the smallest sum?

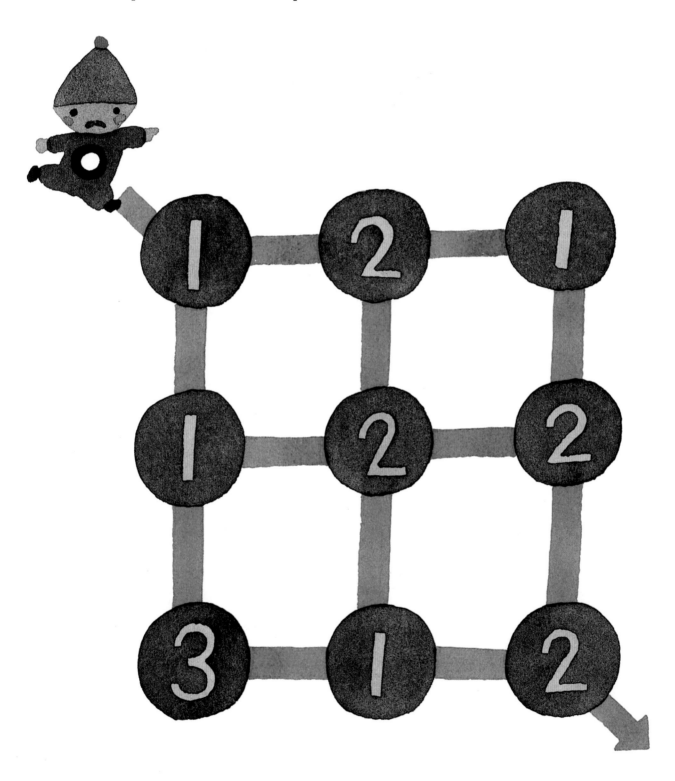

What's wrong with this clock?
What's wrong with this calendar?

1 2 3 4 5
6 7 8 9 10 11 12
13 14 15 16 17 18 19
20 21 22 24 23 25 26
27 28 29 30 31

All of these cubes are the same.

What color is on the bottom of each one?

The **shortest** cap belongs to the dog.

What cap is **second shortest?**

What cap is **tallest?**

If you connect all the pink pipes together and all the green pipes together, which will be longer?

Which is bigger—the blue part or the pink part?

Which is bigger—the orange part or the blue part?

Look carefully! Can you trace the path of the string from one end to the other?

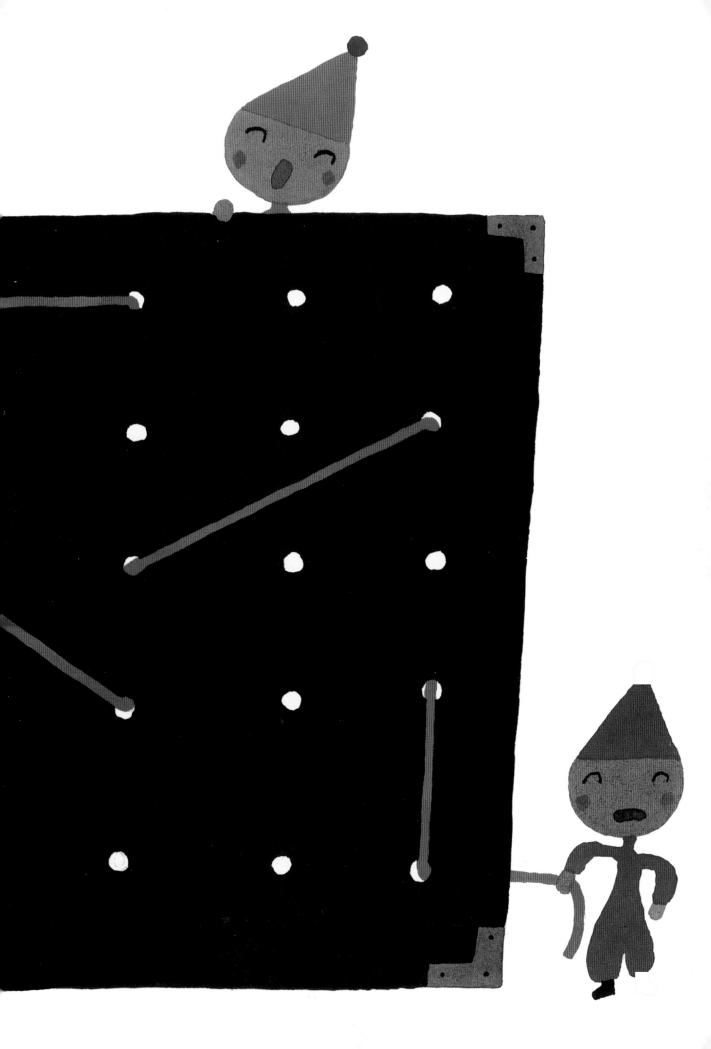

There is a pink square above me, a black square below me, a yellow square to the right, and a blue square to the left. Can you find me?

There is a black square above my friend, a black square below him, a blue square to the right, and a pink square to the left. **Can you find him?**

Watch out!

Which of these kids will fall in the hole?
Which ones won't?

These caterpillars are munching leaves.

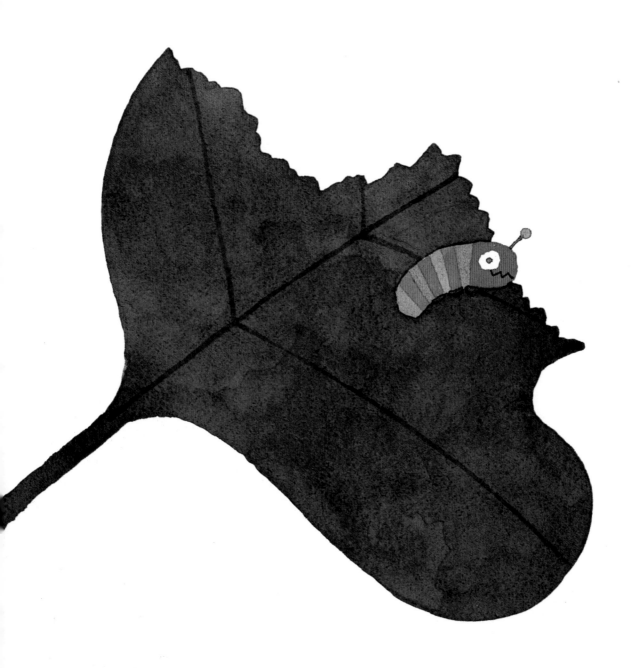

**What shape were the leaves
before they were nibbled?**

A monster! Can you imagine what shape it is under the water?

Or maybe it's two monsters,
or three, or four?

How should they cut this cake into **three pieces?**

How would you cut this cake into **four pieces?**

Will everyone have
a place to sit?

First published in the United States in 2013 by Chronicle Books LLC.

First published in Japan in 1998 and 1999 by KAISEI-SHA Publishing Co., Ltd., Tokyo, under the titles *Sagashitemiyô Mitsuketemiyô* (1998), *Kazoetemiyô, Kurabetemiyô* (1998), *Tameshitemiyô Kangaetemiyô* (1999), *Kangaerunowa Tanoshiine* (1999), *Kotae Iroiro Sutekidane* (1999), and *Umaku Dekiruto Ureshiine* (1999).

English translation rights arranged with KAISEI-SHA Publishing Co., Ltd., Tokyo through Japan Foreign-Rights Centre.

Library of Congress Cataloging-in-Publication Data available.
ISBN 978-1-4521-0839-1

Cover design by Lauren Michelle Smith.
Typeset in Avenir.

Manufactured in China.

10 9 8 7 6 5 4 3 2 1

Chronicle Books LLC
680 Second Street, San Francisco, California 94107

www.chroniclekids.com